KT-471-924

Aspects of P.E.

Taking Part in Sports

Kirk Bizley

Heinemann
LIBRARY

246 781

NORWICH CITY COLLEGE		
Stock No.	246	781
Class	796.06 BIZ	
Cat.		Proc 3WL

www.heinemann.co.uk/library
Visit our website to find out more information about Heinemann Library books.

To order:

 Phone ++44 (0) 1865 888066

 Send a fax to ++44 (0) 1865 314091

 Visit the Heinemann Bookshop at www.heinemann.co.uk/library to browse our catalogue and order online.

First published in Great Britain by Heinemann Library, Halley Court, Jordan Hill, Oxford OX2 8EJ, part of Harcourt Education. Heinemann is a registered trademark of Harcourt Education Ltd.

© Harcourt Education Ltd 1999, 2007
2nd Edition first published in paperback in 2008
The moral right of the proprietor has been asserted.

All rights reserved. No part of this publication may be reproduced, stored in a retrieval system, or transmitted in any form or by any means, electronic, mechanical, photocopying, recording, or otherwise, without either the prior written permission of the publishers or a licence permitting restricted copying in the United Kingdom issued by the Copyright Licensing Agency Ltd, 90 Tottenham Court Road, London W1T 4LP (www.cla.co.uk).

Editorial: Andrew Farrow
Design: Joanna Hinton-Malivoire
Picture research: Hannah Taylor
Production: Alison Parsons

Originated by Dot Gradations Ltd
Printed and bound in China by CTPS

ISBN 978 0 4310 7880 9 (hardback)
11 10 09 08 07
10 9 8 7 6 5 4 3 2 1

ISBN 978 0 4310 7887 8 (paperback)
12 11 10 09 08
10 9 8 7 6 5 4 3 2 1

British Library Cataloguing in Publication Data
Bizley, Kirk
Taking part in Sports. – 2nd ed. – (Aspects of P.E.)
796'.01
A full catalogue record for this book is available from the British Library.

Acknowledgements
The publishers would like to thank the following for permission to reproduce photographs:
Action Plus pp. **7** (R. Francis), **25** (Glyn Kirk), **42** (Chris Barry), **43** (R. Francis); Agence Vandystadt (Stephanie Kempinaire) p. **12**; Allsport pp. **31** (Clive Brunskill), **33** (Ben Radford), **38** (Steve Morton); ASP p. **30**; Coloursport pp. **8** (Max Collin), **19**, **24**; Corbis pp. **9** (Christian Liewig), **17** (Schlegelmilch), **22** (EPA/Gerry Penny), **27** (Reuters/Sergio Perez); Empics (Ross Kinnaird) p. **35**; Getty Images pp. **13**, **21** (Phil Cole), **26** (Mike Hewitt), **36** (Bongarts/Christof Koepsel); Mike Brett Photography pp. **4**, **5**, **32**; Patrick Eager Photography p. **14**; Rex Features p. **15**; Robert Harding Picture Library pp. **20** (Andrew Robinson), **29** (G. Boutin); Topfoto.co.uk p. **23**.

Cover photograph of Kelly Smith of England, at a 2006 Women's World Cup qualifier match, reproduced with permission of Getty Images (Ian Walton).

The author and publishers would like to thank Nuala Mullan and Doug Neate for their comments in the preparation of the first edition of this book.

Every effort has been made to contact copyright holders of any material reproduced in this book. Any omissions will be rectified in subsequent printings if notice is given to the publishers.

Disclaimer
All the Internet addresses (URLs) given in this book were valid at the time of going to press. However, due to the dynamic nature of the Internet, some addresses may have changed, or sites may have changed or ceased to exist since publication. While the author and publishers regret any inconvenience this may cause readers, no responsibility for any such changes can be accepted by either the author or the publishers.

To mum, with thanks for everything.

Contents

1   Facilities 4

2   Sponsorship. 12

3   How sport is financed. 20

4   Attitudes to sports and games. 24

5   Discrimination in sport 28

6   The role of spectators 34

7   What makes people take part? 40

     Glossary. 46

     Find out more 47

     Index. 48

Any words appearing in the text in bold, **like this**, are explained in the Glossary.

Taking part in sport is often determined by the availability of the proper facilities, and these vary considerably.

- *Outdoor facilities* – include sports pitches, water-sports areas, outdoor pursuit areas, and any natural features that might be used for outdoor sporting events, such as cross-country courses. Natural features such as hills have even led to specific sports such as hill runs.

- *Indoor facilities* – are usually purpose built for certain sports (such as swimming pools and fitness gyms) or built to cater for a variety of sports (sports halls or leisure centres).

Outdoor facilities

Some sporting activities depend upon certain natural features such as seas, lakes or particular landscapes. If this is the case, people who want to take part have to travel to the natural site because it is not always possible to build artificial facilities near to where people live.

Sports, such as skiing, even need particular climatic conditions as well as suitable landscapes. Although it may be possible to build a dry ski slope, it is impossible to build an entire artificial snow-covered mountainside!

For most sports, however, you just need an available space, preferably of flat land, where a pitch – or pitches – can be laid down, prepared and maintained. Increasingly, artificial surfaces are being used, but even these need a suitable flat and accessible area.

Facilities for a sport that is played on a natural surface such as grass must be situated outdoors, otherwise the grass will not grow. Other activities, such as cross-country running, need such a large area that it would not be possible to enclose it all indoors. Cricket also requires a very large playing area and it has never been possible to build a suitable indoor stadium. Instead, a version of the game has been developed for indoor play.

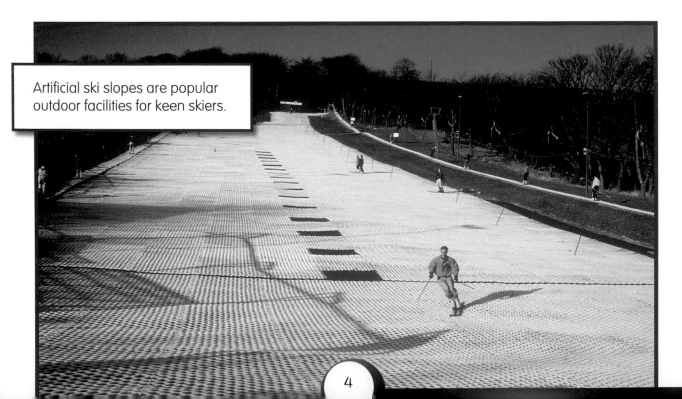

Artificial ski slopes are popular outdoor facilities for keen skiers.

Many inland water areas are being used for a variety of water sports.

Land is expensive, especially in inner city or **urban areas**, so many outdoor facilities are located out of towns. Many existing sports facilities are now being relocated to the outskirts of towns where there is better access. The owners of the inner-city sites are getting high prices for the original grounds, but there is growing pressure on landowners, both in inner cities and out of town, to use their land for more profitable things such as property development.

Making the most of outdoor areas

There have been initiatives recently that focus on making more use of outdoor areas. Many disused quarries and gravel pits, for example, have been flooded and turned into lakes to allow for the increased interest in water-based sports such as windsurfing, jet-skiing, waterskiing and sailing.

Many people use outdoor areas for other leisure-based activities such as rambling, walking or mountain biking. These are easy to start and comparatively cheap to do, which is one of their main attractions.

Because of the uncertain British climate, it is not always easy to get spectators to many outdoor events, especially if they can't be held in outdoor sports stadiums. Bad weather such as heavy frosts, snow, strong winds or rain can even result in the activities being cancelled. This can certainly put a lot of people off going to watch. Some sports, however, such as the major golfing championships, do attract very large numbers of spectators. This is no doubt due, in part, to the fact that these events occur during the summer months.

Indoor facilities

Indoor activities do have a major advantage over outdoor sports: there is more choice in terms of where you can locate indoor facilities. However, there are still many factors that have to be taken into consideration. It is common for the people funding these facilities to carry out quite extensive surveys before they make a final decision about location. They need to consider carefully:

• *Population and expected use* – there is no point in building a facility if there is no one around to use it. Therefore, most of the major indoor facilities are built in areas with a large population, which means there are plenty of potential customers. The cost of running any facility is very high and large numbers of people are needed to use it regularly to make it financially worthwhile.

More and more specialist indoor facilities for athletics events are being provided. Good indoor facilities mean that sports can be practised and competed in regardless of weather conditions.

- *Access* – people need to be able to reach the facility. People using the facility may be travelling by foot, road, rail or even aeroplane. This would be an important factor if it was hoped to host any international events in the facility. Transport links would need to be considered and, if necessary, provided or improved. This would need the support of the local authority and perhaps national government departments.

  Access for people with disabilities should also be considered, for example providing ramps leading into a facility and ramps or lifts within it.

- *Parking* – this is one of the most important factors, as many users would probably travel to a facility by car or coach. There must be suitable and adequate parking space available for the people using the facility, as well as for staff working there.

- *Cost* – this has a number of aspects. The cost of actually building the facility may not be as important a consideration as the cost of purchasing the site to build it on. The building cost will be much the same wherever it is located, but the price of the land can vary considerably. This will often be a major factor in considering the location of a facility.

- *Natural features* – factors such as good drainage or climate may be very important when locating a stadium.

  An area on a steep slope may be ideal if someone wants to build a dry ski-slope and make use of the natural landscape, but it would not be very good for laying out sports pitches that need a flat, level surface.

- *Demand* – if the facility is specific to a particular activity, there would need to be sufficient demand for the activity in that particular area to justify building it.

- *Competition and rival facilities* – there is no point in providing a facility if a similar one already exists – unless the demand is greater than can be satisfied by what is already on offer. In a heavily populated area, several sports halls might be well used, but including a swimming pool or ice rink with each of them is unlikely to be worthwhile. Running costs of a facility increase, as more variety is offered. There is probably not a swimming pool in the UK that actually makes money – they are all **subsidized** by the other facilities they are attached to.

- *Flexibility and versatility* – it will be an advantage if the facility can be used for a variety of activities. Some activities become popular as a result of a trend. If a facility is built specifically for such an activity, it can become a problem if the interest drops away. This is why leisure centres are usually the main providers of facilities because they are flexible in what they can offer. A large hall can be used for indoor activities such as football, hockey, badminton and basketball, and also for displays, conferences, and even concerts.

- *Dual use* – many school sites are **dual use** so it makes sense to locate the facility where it can be used by the public and a school at different times, rather than duplicating the facility within the same area. This is an important consideration and it is often worthwhile – and certainly cheaper – to consider updating or improving existing facilities rather than attempting to build brand new ones.

Many hotels provide their own private facilities for their guests to use.

Providers of facilities

Facilities may be provided by:

- the **private sector**

- the **public sector**.

There may be very distinct differences in the ways in which these facilities are provided.

Private sector

Any type of facility that is run and owned by individuals, firms or companies falls into this category. The facilities have to be run as businesses because the main aim of providing them is to make money.

This type of facility includes:

- health clubs

- hotels with sports facilities such as swimming pools, fitness suites, small gyms or even outdoor facilities such as tennis courts

- holiday camps

- Outward Bound centres

- riding schools.

In addition there are also many clubs that are run privately and are owned either by the members or by companies.

These include some of the major facilities within the UK, such as:

- football stadiums and grounds
- rugby grounds
- golf clubs
- tennis clubs
- bowls clubs
- squash clubs
- sports stadiums (such as Wembley)
- venues that stage large sporting events, such as Wembley Arena, Birmingham International Conference Centre and the Albert Hall.

One thing that all of these facilities have in common is that they must make money, or at least **break even** financially. Clubs are usually happy to break even, because their main function is to provide the facility for their members. They do not usually need to employ many staff, as many jobs are done by the members.

In contrast, the larger companies want to make large profits. They probably have to spend a lot of money paying staff and for the upkeep of their facilities. Some of the major football clubs, such as Manchester United, Liverpool and Tottenham Hotspur, have been or are **public limited companies (plcs)** that have **shareholders**. More and more professional sports clubs are choosing to follow this path because they find it the most profitable way to run the business. This means that they are major companies, just like many others that may not even be connected with sport. They are expected to make money and to pay some of their profits to shareholders in the form of **dividends**.

Major sports facilities can have a huge effect on the local community. Arsenal football club had to work with other private organizations and public bodies to build its new Emirates Stadium.

Public sector

Public sector facilities are owned and run by local authorities or councils. They do not run a private membership scheme. People still have to pay to use these facilities, but they are open to everyone. They include:

- leisure centres
- sports halls
- swimming pools
- sports pitches and courts
- schools
- town halls (and even village halls).

All of these are financed by the taxes paid by local people, which are collected to provide amenities in their area. Some of the money goes to pay for road maintenance, street lighting and a great many other things that are essential for the local community. In recent years the provision of sporting and leisure facilities has been given some priority as people have recognized their benefit.

The cost of building these facilities is very high. A swimming pool, for example, costs several million pounds to design and build, and thousands of pounds a year to run. These high costs are caused by the complicated procedure needed to heat, clean and maintain the pool itself, as well as wages for the very high number of staff who are needed to manage the pool and ensure that it is supervised by qualified people at all times. This may explain why there is not a publicly run swimming pool that actually makes money.

How is it, then, that these facilities get built in the first place and then manage to stay open? The answer is that they are subsidized by the local authority (and therefore by the local taxpayers) and kept going even though they may be losing money. This also explains how facilities are able to keep their fees quite low. There may even be arrangements for especially low rates for certain members of the community such as:

- people who are unemployed
- people receiving certain national benefits or assistance
- young people
- senior citizens
- disabled people
- people recommended to use some sporting facilities under the **GP referrals system**.

All local authorities aim to provide facilities for the people in their area, although it is a discretionary requirement (which means that it is not required by law). In some areas sporting and leisure facilities are given high priority and a great deal of money is spent.

Doctor's orders

Patients are being prescribed exercise as a form of treatment from their family doctors and being sent to local leisure centres to make use of the specialist staff and facilities there. Some patients are also being prescribed memberships of organized slimming clubs to help them lose weight and adopt healthy eating habits.

The fact that local authorities are able to subsidize facilities means that they often provide a great deal, as they do not expect to make money. This is why there are very few privately owned swimming pools at leisure centres in the UK. The building and running costs would be too great ever to allow a profit to be made.

One problem that can arise is that people living in **rural areas** do not have the same access to leisure facilities as the people living in large cities or towns. The facilities that are available are often scaled down. If people in rural areas wish to use a major facility they may have to travel quite a long way to do so. Local authorities in highly populated areas often have very large budgets and are therefore more able to spend money on bigger and better facilities.

Leisure and recreation facilities

Leisure time is the time when you are free to do what you choose. To many people this is the time when they are not at work or at school. Not all of this time is available for you to choose what to do. There are various essentials that must be taken into account, such as sleeping and eating, and you may have to spend a certain amount of time doing household jobs and travelling. The time left after all of this is your leisure time.

Recreation can mean just relaxing or amusing yourself, but it often means something that is active and healthy. Being active is certainly something that you can do in your leisure time! Recreation has been called 'the purposeful use of leisure time' and this is quite a good definition.

Leisure and recreation can cover a wide variety of activities. Facilities for these activities can include:

- parks and public play areas

- skateboard ramps

- cinemas

- tenpin bowling alleys

- public houses (these are the main providers for many organized activities such as cribbage leagues, darts, skittles, pool, quizzes and other recognized 'pub games')

- nightclubs

- theatres

- meeting places for uniformed organizations such as the Scout and Guides Associations, army cadets or the Territorial Army

- youth clubs.

There will almost certainly continue to be a great demand for leisure and recreation facilities because of:

- *greater automation at work and at home* – there are more machines that are capable of doing jobs that used to take a long time. Labour-saving devices such as washing machines and dishwashers leave individuals more time

- *shorter working week* – the average working week is now considerably shorter than it was in the past

- *public awareness about the need for a healthier lifestyle* – the government and media often focus on healthier living, encouraging people of all ages to become fitter and more active.

2) Sponsorship

Sponsorship is increasingly common in sport, although it has developed comparatively recently.

What is sponsorship?

A business or other organization may be persuaded to pay all or some of the expenses of a team or individual player. In return, the business has the benefit of being associated with the good image of the sport and the team or the player being sponsored.

What gets sponsored?

The range of sponsorship now covers individuals, teams or clubs, or even entire sports or events. It is very rare to find any aspect of sport where there is not some form of sponsorship.

Individuals

It is not just people involved in individuals' sports who are sponsored. It is increasingly common for individuals within a team to arrange and negotiate their own sponsorship deals. In fact, a growing number of **agents** act for these individuals by negotiating with the sponsors to arrange the best deal possible.

Most professional sportspeople are sponsored, often by more than one company. For example, a racing driver's car and racing overalls are often covered with names of sponsors and their products. Each of the sponsors pays a substantial amount for that advertising space.

Some sports are more popular than others and are therefore more appealing to the sponsors. This puts the players in that sport in a very good bargaining position.

Basketball has a very large worldwide appeal and some of the individual players have their own sponsorship arrangements, while there are separate arrangements for the team as a whole. This can sometimes lead to conflicts and there have been cases where clashes have occurred between what the individual may choose to wear and what the team are expected to wear.

Sportsplayers who are particularly successful can be paid very large amounts of money. They may actually have companies queuing up to sponsor them, and making rival bids through agents. It can reach the stage where sports players receive more money from their sponsorship deals than they do from taking part in the sport itself.

Many individuals from team sports such as basketball and football also negotiate their own personal sponsorship deals.

Important events attract major sponsorship. Meeting the needs of major sponsors, including personal sponsors, can put pressure on top stars such as young US golfer Michelle Wie, shown here.

Teams and clubs

At just about any level, from small local football teams to full international teams, there is a great deal of sponsorship. Particularly successful teams can attract a great deal of sponsorship, which can have huge benefits.

Sometimes small firms and businesses will sponsor local teams. This is a very good system because the small teams are not able to attract major sponsors, and small firms or businesses cannot afford to spend sufficient money on deals with the very large clubs.

The clubs may have more than one team (this is often the case, for example, with rugby clubs) and they may be able to arrange different sponsors for the different teams, or one sponsor may agree to sponsor all of the teams.

Sports

Sometimes the sport itself is sponsored, or its controlling association (usually the **national**

governing body) arranges a sponsorship deal. This means that all of the members of the association, including all the clubs and their members, can enjoy the benefits.

Sponsors often choose sports with a good image, and they are happy to help the whole sport nationally and not in just one particular area. The major sports are also prime targets for the sponsors because of their popularity and high profile generally. None of the major sports seem to have any difficulty in attracting sponsors, but some of the **minority sports** may find it more difficult.

Events

Sponsorship of particular events has become very popular because the sponsors are guaranteed to be associated with successful teams. If they take charge of the whole event they do not have to take the risk that an individual, or a team, might fail. As long as the event or competition goes smoothly, they are guaranteed a lot of advertising space and publicity.

All sorts of events are sponsored, from local gymnastic championships through to major international events such as the Olympic Games. In the case of the Olympics, the event is so big that no one sponsor alone can pay the large amounts of money required. Because of this there are many sponsors, usually from the large **multinational companies**, that can benefit from their products being seen all over the world.

If an event is well sponsored then the **organizers** can guarantee that it will be a financial success because of the sponsors' involvement alone. In the past organizers had to rely on making money from the entry fees and from the people who would actually go along to watch the event and pay admission charges. The great increase in sponsorship is one of the reasons why there are now more and more competitions and events in nearly all of the sports that are available.

Types of sponsorship

Sponsorship can take many forms. It originally started in the days when there was a lot more **amateur** sport. Then it was a way of helping a sportsperson without directly giving them money – as this was not allowed. Now it takes place in all of the following areas.

Equipment

As part of a sponsorship arrangement, a sportsperson may be given all of their equipment for their chosen sport. This equipment is usually manufactured by the sponsoring company and could range from sports shoes to rackets, and perhaps specialist training equipment. Even at a lower level of competition some sportspeople are offered their equipment at reduced prices or agreed **terms**. This encourages them to use a particular brand of equipment.

Clothing

Clothing sponsorship can include not only the clothing that is worn for taking part in sport, but also extra items such as sunglasses or baseball caps with the manufacturer's name on them. In some sports there are even rules that say how large the manufacturer's logo can be on the clothing and even where it may actually be displayed. Tennis has a rule that states only two small patches may be used on a player's shirt to advertise a product that is not directly linked to tennis or tennis equipment.

Sportspeople such as cricketers can even be sponsored to wear sunglasses!

Accessories

Some firms or companies are prepared to pay for their products to be worn, even if they have no direct link to the sport. This is why many tennis players are sponsored to wear certain watches (which can be seen on television as the player serves) and cricketers are paid to wear branded sunglasses.

Transport and travel

Transport and travel costs are often paid for and, in some cases, even provided by sponsors. Car firms may provide free cars, often with drivers, for competitions. Air travel companies may provide free flights. It is quite common for the top world-class tennis players to be flown to all their international tournaments by one of their national airlines.

Even at lower levels, coach companies may provide free (or reduced rate) transport, and local garages may provide cars and/or petrol.

Accommodation

Many sports performers find themselves constantly travelling from one competition to another and they always have to stay near the competition base. Therefore help with accommodation is very important. The top performers can often make arrangements with leading hotel chains throughout the world.

Money

Some performers receive sponsorship in the form of cash payments, so they can decide exactly what to spend it on. If all the other costs of their sporting career are covered then this just becomes an extra source of income.

Training

Training can be sponsored in several ways. Performers may have facilities provided or paid for, or paid time off work may be arranged to enable them to receive extra training. In some sports, such as tennis, individual players are provided with personal trainers or coaches. Specialist training equipment may even be installed and provided for the performer.

Many sportspeople receive major sponsorship. They can also earn money from other commercial opportunities. In 2006 footballer Ashley Cole and singer Cheryl Tweedy helped launch a new National Lottery game.

Entry fees and expenses

Fees paid to enter events can soon mount up and become very expensive, especially to a newcomer in a sport. Performers might get into a situation where they cannot afford to pay entry fees for events in which they must compete to further their career.

Food

Food is another very common type of sponsorship. There are many examples of butchers sponsoring field-event athletes who need specific nutrients in their diet, which they may get from eating large amounts of meat.

Benefits for sponsors

Sponsorship obviously has benefits to the sponsors or there would be no point in offering it. The benefits can be considerable and fall into the following broad areas.

Advertising

Sponsoring a sports performer is one of the most effective ways of advertising a product or service. It can also work out cheaper than many other forms of advertising such as television adverts, newspapers, or radio. It has the added advantage that the event, or the performer, may be shown on television, so that the sponsor gets wider coverage.

Some products are not allowed to be directly advertised on television (for example cigarettes and other tobacco products), so sponsorship had been a way to avoid this ban. This is why so many of the televised snooker tournaments were sponsored by tobacco companies, because they saw this as a way of getting around the rules. However, tobacco sponsorship finally ended in 2003.

Some sports **governing bodies** already forbid their sports to be associated with manufacturers of tobacco products or alcoholic drinks.

Tax relief

Sponsors can claim their sponsoring expenses against the tax that they have to pay. This means that sponsorship can actually save the sponsors money.

Image

Sport can present a good image as it can show a healthy, successful lifestyle. Association with this image is good for companies and products and it can raise the standing of their products with the public. This has proved to be the case with a lot of sportswear, where the image of the designer label has become very important, and it has been equally important to link it to a successful sports performer.

Research and development

Manufacturers persuade performers to use their existing products and they also get them to try out some of their new ones. Just as car manufacturers test-drive new vehicles before they are put into production, so manufacturers of sports goods try out their new equipment before deciding to produce it

Sportswear

Manufacturers of sportswear only expect a small percentage of their products to be worn for actual sporting use. The majority of sales are as fashion items and for leisure wear.

on a large scale. Many of the new materials currently in use have been tried out in this way, but not all of them have been successful.

Goodwill

Although this is very closely linked with image, many sponsors are prepared to help as a gesture of **goodwill** – without any guarantees that they will gain from it. This is often the case at the lowest level of sponsorship, in helping out small local teams and individuals.

Sponsor requests

The Australian cricketer, Denis Lillee, at a sponsor's request, once went out to bat with a cricket bat made of tin! It was not successful and was actually banned by the cricketing authorities. It was only ever used that one time.

Formula One cars, such as this Renault driven by Fernando Alonso, carry the logos of their many sponsors. There are strict rules in Europe about the brands and products that can be marketed at televised races.

Improved sales

Probably the single most important benefit to any sponsor is improved sales. If they have to pay money out in some form, a sponsor will wish to get as much back as possible in terms of increased sales of their product. Successful sponsorship has proven to guarantee this. Vast sums of money can be generated if the right kind of sponsorship deals are negotiated.

Sponsorship and the media

For sponsorship to be fully successful at the highest level, it is very important to have strong links with all forms of the **media**. It is through the media that sponsors are able to have their involvement fully recognized. Television is, perhaps, the most important of the media forms for advertising, and the sponsors have made various arrangements to make sure that they are able to take full advantage of their sponsorship deals. Sponsors take advantage of media coverage of sporting events in several ways:

• *Billboards and advertising* – whatever the size of the venue where the event is taking place, there will be strategically placed advertising. It may be just behind the place where snooker players sit down when they are not playing, or all around the perimeter of a football pitch.

Computer-designed graphics are even drawn on to the playing surfaces so that they can be seen by the TV cameras and given a 3D effect. These are used at many cricket grounds and rugby grounds. The organizers will always be contacted to ensure that the TV cameras are positioned so maximum exposure can be maintained.

• *Sponsored programmes and events* – sometimes the sponsors will actually pay to have a programme broadcast in their name. This is very common with the satellite networks, where certain sports programmes are linked throughout with a reference to a firm or manufacturer. Golf, football and basketball programmes are often associated with one particular manufacturer and the commentators and broadcasters have to make constant references to them.

Advantages and disadvantages of sponsorship deals

Advantages

• Young and promising players and performers are able to concentrate on their sport with fewer financial worries.

• Sport can be promoted and encouraged so that participation levels increase.

• The image of sport can be improved by a partnership with a company that has a good image.

Sponsor 'time outs'

In the United States, it is common to have 'time outs' (breaks in play) to give sponsors the required amount of advertising slots. In games of American football, the TV producers actually contact the officials on the field directly to stop play when they want to!

- More money is provided for the sport to pay for administration, facilities, coaching, training and improving standards.

- Bigger and better events can be staged and organized.

- Award schemes can be paid for and advertised.

- New and minority sports can be encouraged and financed.

- Competitions and leagues can be run, with the provision of prizes and finance.

- Sponsors can get many benefits (see pages 16–18).

Disadvantages

- The sport can lose its own identity and be overly influenced by the sponsors.

- Rules can be changed at the sponsor's request. This is particularly so in the case of what is considered appropriate sportswear, and sometimes the length of time the event is to last. This happens more in large-scale events and competitions so it can often affect the sport at the very highest level.

- The timing of events is often dictated by the sponsors – particularly when the sport is being televised. Times are chosen to suit an international audience (this usually means the United States as they traditionally provide the highest viewing figures for international sporting events), and these may not be in the best interests of the performer or the sport.

- Less popular sports and performers do not attract or receive as much sponsorship and this clearly affects their development.

- Products that have a negative image, such as unhealthy foods or types of alcohol, can damage a sport in terms of its reputation and image.

- If a sponsor has to withdraw, the sport or performer may not be able to continue.

- The sport may become over commercialized – reducing the fun aspect of taking part for the participants.

Tobacco sponsorship used to be common at sporting events. It is now banned in the UK because health professionals believe it encourages people to link smoking with a healthy lifestyle.

BENSON and HEDGES MASTERS

Sport needs funding to provide facilities and activities. It also needs money in order to be well organized, and so that we can enjoy sport as a form of entertainment and **recreation**. The most costly of these are the facilities (see Chapter 1). Sport needs money, but how is the money raised or provided?

Amateur clubs

Throughout the country there are many thousands of clubs that not only provide sporting opportunities but also finance them all. They raise this money in several ways:

- *Membership fees* – every member pays a set amount each year to belong to the club. This is also known as a **subscription** (or **subs**). Members also pay a match fee each time they play a game or match.

- *Fund-raising* – most clubs hold social events, sponsored events, car boot sales and any other functions they can think of to raise money. The vast majority of them also have some sort of social area, or bar, where they provide drinks and refreshments for the members. For many small clubs this will be the main source of income. The profits made here help to keep the club going.

- *Grants* – some money comes from grants from local authorities or national bodies such as the **Sports Council** or the **governing body** of their particular sport.

- *Sponsorship* – this is becoming increasingly important (see Chapter 2).

Charities

Many sports associations are registered as charities. This means that they gain either exemption from paying tax or at least some reduction in the taxes they have to pay. In addition the organization may well be more successful in obtaining grants or sponsorship.

Professional clubs

In many sports there are professional clubs that are run as businesses and have to raise all of their own finance. They need to make money to pay their players' wages, and they may have to pay large sums of money to 'sign' new players. This is probably their largest single expenditure (apart from their facilities, if they own these themselves) and can involve spending millions of pounds just to buy one player!

Car boot sales can be a way to raise money for a small club.

Professional clubs have two major sources of income:

• *Spectators* – if the club has a large stadium it can raise a lot of money from people paying to watch matches. Many clubs sell **season tickets**, so supporters pay in advance for a ticket that entitles them to watch all of their team's home games. Using this method, many of the most successful teams can sell tickets in advance for nearly all the games for a season. Luxury executive boxes (specially situated viewing areas) have also been introduced. Companies can buy or hire these boxes, and then invite the clients they are entertaining to watch a match. Most clubs now have these boxes and it is always a priority to provide them, if any ground changes or improvements are being made.

Andriy Schevchenko

When Chelsea paid AC Milan £30 million in 2006 for Andriy Shevchenko it made him the most expensive signing in professional British sport.

• **Merchandizing** – this is the sale of goods or items associated with the club. The goods can range from coffee mugs, scarves and duplicate shirts, to programmes, posters or sports equipment. This is a very large and important source of income for the big, successful clubs and is also a growth area. Manchester United football club has its own 'megastores' throughout the country and estimates that half of its annual income comes from merchandizing.

Shirt sponsorship is a major source of income for football teams. Chelsea's team sponsor for the 2006–07 season, for example, was worth more than £50 million over a 5-year period.

David Beckham

When David Beckham first joined Real Madrid the club's income that season from merchandizing rose 67 per cent to £33.8 million!

Governing bodies

The governing body of a sporting activity receives money and can raise money. All the clubs and individuals who belong to the particular sport have to pay a subscription, and part of this goes to the governing body. The payment often covers things such as insurance (a very important factor with a lot of the martial arts sports, for example) but some money can be made available for coaching and preparing teams.

Governing bodies can also raise money through organizing and running events, competitions and tournaments. For many of them this is the biggest money-earner of them all, especially if they have a well established and successful tournament for which they are responsible. The Lawn Tennis Association, for example, makes millions of pounds each year from the Wimbledon tennis tournament and much of this money is put back into the sport by providing facilities, coaching and promotion for the sport. It is this money that helps to provide personal coaches and trainers for the most promising new players, to help them with their development.

The Rugby Football Union also receives large sums of money for staging international games. This money is then available to be distributed amongst the many clubs that are members. It has been used to finance improvements to the stadium at Twickenham, to make it one of the most modern in the UK.

National and local government

A great deal of money is raised each year through national and local taxes. Some of this is spent providing sporting facilities and generally financing sport. Much of the money is available through grants.

To obtain a grant for a particular purpose, a sporting body has to make a specific application to whichever agency has been appointed by the Government to administer the funds. An agency such as UK Sport receives money directly from the Government and then has to consider each of the separate applications that it receives for financial help. There are specific guidelines and limits for the type of help that is available. The agency may consider specific sports as well as applications from sporting individuals.

Sponsorship

Vast amounts of money are provided for sport each year by sponsorship deals. Sponsorship provides money for all aspects of sport, at all levels, and is possibly the largest and most important

Some of the revenue from the Wimbledon tennis tournament is put back into the sport. Sources of this revenue include ticket sales, sponsorship, and fees for televised matches such as the 2006 final between Amelie Mauresmo and Justine Henin-Hardenne.

single source of finance. It is certainly one of the priority areas and is considered very carefully by any sporting organization.

Gambling

Gambling has been linked with sporting events for many years. It is one of the principal reasons why horse racing exists – for many people there would be very little appeal in horse racing were it not for the process of placing a bet on the outcome of a race.

Other sports, such as football, also have very close links with gambling. The football pools companies pay the sport a great deal of money to be allowed to use the results of the league matches to decide who wins the jackpot every weekend. To some people the pools value of the result is even more important than whether their own football team has won or lost. The amount of money that the pools firms put back into the sport must not be underestimated. It was as a direct result of extra pools companies' money being made available to the clubs that many of the professional clubs were able to improve the conditions and facilities in their grounds, following the publication of the **Taylor Report**. This report recommended upgrading the safety measures in football stadiums.

The National Lottery (which was launched in 1994) has had a significant effect upon the financing of sport. Sport was specifically identified as one of the areas that should benefit from any money raised by the lottery and, in a comparatively short time, many millions of pounds have been made available. Organizations – large and small – can **bid** for money, and many new facilities have already been provided as a result. These sums of money were simply not available in the past, so this is going to be a great benefit for many years to come.

The media

Many sports authorities deal directly with the **media** (especially television) to negotiate the fees for covering their sport. With the introduction and growth of satellite television there is now far more competition and more money to be made. Because of increased coverage all sports, not just the major ones, can gain.

The National Lottery is a major fund-raiser for sport.

All physical activities have some rules or regulations that people taking part must follow. Having a good sporting attitude means playing within those rules or regulations and being totally fair – even to the point where it could cost you the game. A poor sporting attitude, sometimes called **gamesmanship**, is the opposite of this, and it often comes very close to cheating.

When you take part in sport you have many moral decisions to make and one of the most important of these is how fairly you decide to play.

Good sporting attitude

There have been many sporting performers who have been called great sportspeople, but not all of them have actually shown the necessary qualities or attitudes. Unfortunately, many sporting characters have achieved fame through having a poor attitude, as it encouraged spectators to attend their performances, sometimes in the hope that they would do something outrageous. Some of these performers acted in this way because it was what the spectators expected and wanted.

Most sports have accepted ways in which a good attitude can be displayed:

• *Football* – if a player is injured another player (even on the opposing team) might kick the ball out of play. This is so that the game can be stopped and the injured player can receive some medical attention. When the game is then restarted you can throw or kick the ball back to the team who kicked it out, so that you do not gain an unfair advantage.

• *Racket games* – there are such things as **sling shots** and **double hits** that a player making a shot can sense and feel, but it is very difficult, if not impossible, for the official in charge to detect them.

You can call out to indicate to your opponent when you make these shots, because they are actually foul shots and are not allowed by the rules of the games. In tennis and squash it is sometimes very difficult to identify a bump ball (where the ball hits

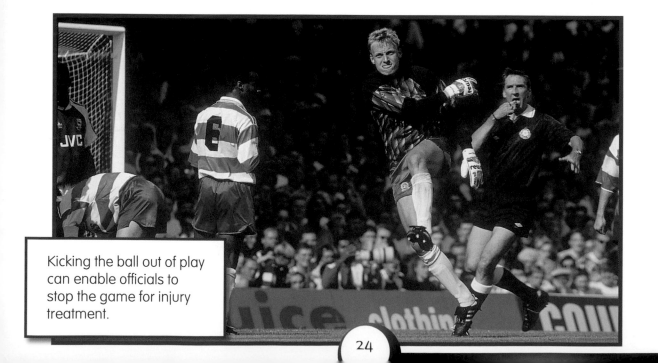

Kicking the ball out of play can enable officials to stop the game for injury treatment.

the ground just before you make contact) and this is something that can also be pointed out to an official or an opponent. Even warming up, prior to a game, by practising shots with an opponent, can be much more helpful if players give their opponents a range of shots to play rather than practising winning shots all of the time.

- *Rugby* – one of the oldest sporting traditions in rugby is to form a tunnel with your team and applaud the other team off the pitch. This should happen no matter how the match went, whether you win or lose. Each team usually does it to the other. It often follows the captains leading their teams in 'three cheers for the opposition', as the final whistle is blown. This tradition also applies in netball and hockey.

- *Cricket* – a batsperson can be applauded on their way to the crease to bat. They may also '**walk**' when they know that they are out, if they have touched the ball with their bat and a fair catch is made. They should not wait for the umpire's decision but should start to walk back to the pavilion. Fielders can also play their part by being honest about whether a ball has carried for a fair catch and if they place any part of their body on or over the boundary rope when fielding. It is also accepted practice at cricket to applaud good batting shots and certainly to congratulate a batter who scores 50 or 100 runs.

- *Golf* – this is a game that relies very heavily on individual players being both honest and fair when playing. They should always admit to the number of shots played, whether or not they might have touched the ball when 'addressing' it, or even to grounding their club if playing in a bunker.

Sometimes simple actions such as helping an opposing player to his feet can be a sign of a good sporting attitude.

The size of a golf course and the large number of rules that apply make good sporting attitude essential for anyone who takes up the game.

General sporting attitude

Examples of good sporting attitude that apply to most sporting activities include:

- welcoming your opposition players

- congratulating opponents on good play

- shaking hands after a game, particularly with the officials

- accepting the decisions of the officials without argument or dispute

- playing fairly and honestly to the rules of the sport.

'Point scoring'

Unfortunately, there are far too many examples of poor sporting attitude, or 'point scoring', for them all to be listed here. There was a famous book, written in 1947 by Stephen Potter, called *The Theory and Practice of Gamesmanship*, in which he defined it as 'the act of winning games without actually cheating'. Sadly, for many people who take part in sport, this is how they do approach the game. 'Point scoring' also occurs at all levels, from the small club player right up to the professional sportsperson. One of the added advantages of the high level of television coverage of sport now is that these practices can be exposed and pressure put on the performers to play fairly.

For some people, it is so important to win that they will try whatever they can to put their opponent off – often by bending the rules or using loopholes in the rules to their own advantage.

Football has had to change its rules because of this. The so-called **professional foul** involved handling the ball, or deliberately fouling an opponent to prevent them from scoring. Although this was against the rules it only resulted in a free kick, or possibly a booking, which was a small price to pay for preventing an opponent from scoring – so it became accepted practice to do it! The rules were therefore changed to make it an automatic sending-off offence in order to deter players from doing it. It has proved to be only partially effective because the practice still goes on. Some players accept being sent off as the price for not conceding a goal!

In cricket, as in many other games, time-wasting is very common practice. A referee

Making the correct field placings are an important part of cricket. Here, Monty Panesar and Andrew Flintoff discuss ideas for getting a Sri Lankan batsman out. Sometimes, however, these discussions can be a form of time-wasting.

in football can add time on or even book an offending player, but in cricket there are no such rules. A team that is playing for a draw has various ways it can waste time including:

• constant field placing changes

• extra long bowler run-ups

• fake injuries or ball checks or inspections

• long drinks intervals.

Slow bowling

In a cricket match in 1967 Brian Close, who was the England cricket captain, managed to get his team, Yorkshire, to bowl only 24 overs in the last 100 minutes. This included taking 15 minutes to bowl the last 2 overs!

Rules have been introduced in cricket to combat slow play and if these rules are broken the punishment is a fine, which the players must pay. Unfortunately slow play tactics still go on. This is mainly due to the fact that it is quite possible, and very common, to have a draw in cricket if the time runs out. This is not possible in a limited overs match and so the problem of slow play does not usually occur.

Another common example of poor sporting attitude in cricket has been the growth of **sledging**. This is where comments are made by the fielding side to the batters to try to put them off their shots. It has reached such high levels in some matches that the umpires have had to meet with the captains. There are moves to introduce new rules to allow the umpires to deal with it more forcefully.

In many sports it is common to 'psyche out' the opponent. This happens particularly in boxing, where the whole process can start at the weigh-in before the fight and continue right up to the start of the actual contest. It can even go on inside the ring as the referee reminds the boxers of the rules of the contest. It has also been known to occur just before rugby matches, as the players get themselves into an aggressive mood ready to start the match. This sort of aggression can get out of hand and the **governing body** has produced guidelines to deal with it at junior levels.

Time-wasting and delaying tactics such as constantly tying up shoe laces and adjusting equipment or clothing are also very common, and they are usually allowed for within the rules of the sport.

Unsporting behaviour

In 1994 the tennis player Boris Becker was criticized for apparent unsporting behaviour at Wimbledon. He took a great deal of time to prepare himself to receive the serve and then several times turned away for no apparent reason. This was most unsettling for his opponent who was waiting to serve. The umpires were instructed to time him and stick strictly to the time limits allowed between the points by the rules of the game.

A crowd of players argues with a referee, who has just awarded a penalty. Putting pressure on officials to change decisions has been an increasing problem in many sports.

Being unfair or unjustly hostile to someone, whatever the circumstances, is not acceptable. There are examples where it has happened in sport and in some cases it still goes on.

Racial discrimination

Racial discrimination can and does occur, not only because of the colour of a person's skin but also because of their nationality. Many countries have a population made up of more than one race, with conflicts occurring between the different peoples. They may even speak different languages and live in separate areas within the country, so their access to sporting facilities may be completely different. Usually, the origins of racial conflict within a country are political. There have been many such conflicts over the years and these have led to problems in sporting contests.

This has particularly been the case with black and non-white sports performers and athletes. In this sort of situation, the racial groups are often called **ethnic minorities**.

Many of the ethnic minorities that exist are the result of slavery in the 17th century, especially in North America. Thousands of slaves were taken from Africa and transported to North America, mainly as agricultural slave labourers. There were so many slaves that separate laws were brought in that applied only to them. The United States did not abolish slavery until 1865, by which time there was a very large population of African descendents living in the country. The end of slavery was not the end of the problem. It took many years before these people were given anything like equal rights. It was not until the 1960s that the civil rights movement was successful.

One African-American sportsman who suffered under such discrimination was the heavyweight boxer, Jack Johnson. He went on to become the first black heavyweight world champion, but his career was constantly threatened because of his colour and background. He married a white American, which was very much disapproved of, not only by the white society but by his own race as well! Johnson won the world title in Australia in 1908 and it was then arranged for him to fight the previous (white) champion, Jim Jeffries, in 1910. The black and white cultures of the United States were divided in their support. When Johnson won there were race riots and 19 people died as a result. Eleven African Americans were killed, many of them hunted down by white mobs. Johnson was later arrested on some dubious charges. He fled from the United States whilst on bail and continued his fighting career in Europe. He returned to the United States to take part in a controversial fight where, it is alleged, he was paid to lose to the latest 'white hope' heavyweight, Jess Willard, in exchange for having charges against him dropped.

It is not only in the United States that racial discrimination has occurred. It has also been quite common in many parts of the UK. **Minority groups** were denied access to clubs, schools and other organizations because of the colour of their skin. Changes in the law were introduced to prevent this, and since then there has been a great improvement.

At one time it would have been very unusual to find a black professional football player, international athlete or cricketer in the UK. Now it is very common as the barriers have broken down.

Black South Africans were not allowed entry to this fairground during apartheid.

In 1993 football's **governing bodies** started a campaign to 'kick racism out of football'. 'Kick it out' has done much to highlight the problems faced by players from ethnic minorities. Details of the campaign can be found at www.kickitout.org.

Apartheid

Apartheid was an extreme example of discrimination that existed in South Africa. It was a policy of segregation (**apartheid** means 'separateness' in the Afrikaans language). It involved rigid racial division between the governing white minority population and the non-white majority population. South Africa had a long history of racial discrimination and there were even laws passed at the start of the 20th century to restrict black people's rights in land ownership. The apartheid laws were introduced in 1948 and classified people under three major racial groups:

- white
- Bantu (or black Africans)
- coloured (people of mixed descent).

Later, Asians (including Indians and Pakistanis) were added as a fourth category. Everything these different groups did was strictly segregated, which meant there were separate schools, cinemas, living areas and even transport.

Sports facilities were also separate, and black people were allowed very few sporting opportunities.

The rest of the world was very much against this system and there were many political problems internationally. The ruling sporting bodies took their own action and South Africa was banned from the Olympic movement. Most ruling bodies banned any other form of sporting links. The sporting **boycott** on South Africa was an important factor in the pressure that was put upon the country. The apartheid system was finally ended in 1994.

Throughout apartheid there had been very little sporting provision for the so-called lower racial groups within the country. When the South African teams were readmitted to international sport, there were few – if any – black members in their teams. It has taken years for the effects of the apartheid policy to be overcome and for the black competitors to have a realistic representation at sporting events and competitions.

National rights

Not all nations give equal rights to their citizens. There may be discrimination against some members within a society.

In some of the Eastern European countries many potential sports performers are selected, often at a very early age, and either sent to special training schools or put on specific coaching and training courses. This often happened in the former USSR, before there was major political change that brought about the collapse of the former communist states in Eastern Europe.

Because the communist countries operated in such isolation and secrecy, many of their methods of selection and training were not made known to the rest of the world. Sport was valued very highly as a way of showing the value of communism, so there were few limits on how far they would go to achieve success. One of the most famous sprinters of the past, the Russian Valeri Bortzov, was alleged to have been selected and specifically trained – partly using computer technology that identified him as a potentially good sprinter. He was then groomed for this for life.

Gymnastics was another area where the Eastern Europeans excelled. There were various selection and training programmes established to ensure that there was a constant supply of young, mainly female, gymnasts to maintain their dominance. There was very little choice for those who were selected. In fact, they would have considered themselves very fortunate to be chosen.

In Cuba (another communist state), there was a time when only eight sports were made available. This was so that Cuba could achieve high standards and a high international status in those sports on which

In communist countries, the selection and training process for young gymnasts was heavily controlled by the state.

they concentrated. They also established strong links with the Eastern European countries, which supplied them with coaches and coaching assistance in those particular sports. The choice for individuals in these countries was very restricted and was frowned upon by the rest of the world.

This form of selection is known as **elitism** because the same opportunities are not made available to everyone. The system of elitism also exists in other countries in a slightly different form.

In the United States it is very common for talented sportspeople, who are thought to have great potential, to be selected for specialist sports colleges and establishments. It is even possible to take a degree course in golf if you have the right potential and ability!

In other countries it is common for a good sportsperson to join the armed forces, or one of the uniformed organizations, to take up special training and preparation. The breakdown of the barriers between **amateur** and professional sport has now just about stopped this, as there is no longer the need for top sportspeople to do anything other than their sport.

Religion

Many individuals, and countries, have been victims of discrimination on religious grounds.

Some committed Christians will not compete on a Sunday, so if there is a major tournament or event that takes place on that day they will not take part. Many competitors have even withdrawn from Olympic Games events because they took place on a Sunday.

Jewish people were victims of discrimination in Germany in the 1930s when they were treated as second-class citizens. They would not even have been considered for selection for any of the German teams. Hitler even tried to prevent them taking part as members of any of the other teams and this greatly affected the whole organization of the 1936 Olympic games, which were held in Berlin.

Not on Sunday

The British triple jumper Jonathan Edwards was one of the performers who would not compete on a Sunday because of his Christian beliefs. He missed many major championships early in his career.

In some strict Muslim countries women are not allowed to wear certain types of clothes. For example, it would be unacceptable for women to wear athletic running clothing. Women in these countries are therefore discriminated against on religious grounds.

Hassiba Boulmerka, who won the 1,500 metres Olympic gold medal in 1992, caused controversy in her own country by training and performing in shorts. Cultural practice in her home country of Algeria expected a woman to keep her legs and arms covered. Boulmerka decided to leave Algeria after receiving threats against her life.

Several religions restrict women from taking part in certain activities and this can greatly affect their ability to participate fully in sport.

Hassiba Boulmerka – who suffered religious discrimination in her home country.

Women's rugby is becoming more accepted – and more popular.

Sexual discrimination

Sexual discrimination can take many forms in sport, although they may not all be immediately obvious:

- *Fewer events* – many events are held for men only and in many professional sports there are no properly organized women's events. Even if women wished to compete, the opportunities may be restricted.

- *Less prize money* – nearly all events have less prize money for women than they do for men. This has even been justified by some **organizers**. The Wimbledon authorities declared that they were paying less prize money because women only had to play a maximum of three sets, as opposed to the men's five. However, from 2007 men and women have been paid equal prize money at Wimbledon.

- *Lower profile* – women's events are not as well promoted or publicized as those for men, nor do they attract the same degree of sponsorship as many of the men's events do.

- *Women are banned* – in the major contact sports women are banned by the ruling bodies from taking part in the same teams or competitions as men, except at the junior levels. It is rare for women to compete against men on equal terms. Showjumping is one of the few exceptions.

Women's World Cups

The first men's football World Cup was held in 1930, but it was not until 1991 that there was a women's World Cup. In the same year, the first ever rugby women's World Cup took place (England lost to the United States in the final). Cricket had led the way as there were women's matches as early as 1745, and the first cricket women's World Cup was in 1973 where England were the hosts and the eventual winners.

Women officials in football

Wendy Toms made history when she was the assistant referee in the Coca Cola Cup quarter final between Stockport and Southampton. It was the most senior British professional match a woman had ever officiated in. Now, all of the officials at major international women's football tournaments are women.

Despite these advances, sexism in football is still prevalent. In 2006 Luton manager Mike Newell criticized women officials in general and was later fined by the Football Association.

• *Few women appear in administrative roles* – very few women have been able to gain important positions within their sport, and to make their feelings and views felt. This occurs in their own sports as well as those that are traditionally men's sports. It can also apply to being an official.

Social, economic and cultural factors

In many areas, and in whole countries, there is simply a lack of money, so the people who live there have less of everything. This is certainly the case with sporting opportunities. Even in the wealthier countries there are inner city areas that are very poor, and which have few – if any – facilities. Almost certainly the few sporting opportunities that are available will be very basic.

This is why many of these areas have produced very good boxers, basketball players and footballers. These sports do not require expensive facilities. Golf courses, tennis clubs and swimming pools may not be available, so these sports are not an option. It was not until 1996 that the United States had its first African-American professional golfer in Tiger Woods, yet African Americans dominate in many of the other US sports.

Nearly all of the best stadiums and training facilities are in the countries of the richest nations and many performers from other countries have to go there to prepare and train properly.

Certain cultural groups within an area may wish to have their chosen sports available, but they may be denied the facilities because of the cost or because it clashes with the choices of the majority culture. Being born or growing up – in the wrong country can be a handicap to many potential sportspeople.

Some sports require only the most basic facilities.

The role of spectators

Crowd influence

All professional sport has spectators. One of the main points of performing is to play in front of a crowd. Most teams prefer to play at home because it is usually a considerable advantage for them.

There can be several factors that make competing at home an advantage, but two of the major reasons for this are:

• *Familiar surroundings* – the home ground or pitch will be very familiar to the players and it may even have some qualities or peculiarities that they are used to. This could be a slope on the pitch or, in the case of cricket, a particular way that the wicket responds to a form of bowling. Being in the familiar dressing rooms and the fact that the team has not had to travel very far can also be helpful factors.

• *Crowd support* – this will be a major factor. Supporters usually cheer on their own team and try to discourage the opposition. Many players find it very intimidating to play away when they know that the opposing fans will be very critical of them, and of any mistakes that they make. Just the crowd noise itself can be enough to unsettle some players and motivate others.

Behaviour

Although most sports organizations want spectators at their events, unfortunately those spectators do not always behave as they should. This can cause severe problems.

During football matches in the 1970s and 1980s there were a great many incidents involving British fans. These included hooliganism, drunkenness, violence and even riots before, during and after games.

Some record attendances in British football

Highest British football attendance: 149,547, Scotland vs England, Hampden Park, 13 April 1937

Highest league attendance: 83,260, Manchester United vs Arsenal, Division 1, Old Trafford, 17 January 1948

Highest Premier League attendance: 76,073, Manchester United vs Aston Villa, Old Trafford, 13 January 2007

Lowest league attendance: 469, Thames vs Luton Town, Third Division South, West Ham, 6 December 1930

Lowest Premier League attendance: 3,039, Wimbledon vs Everton, Selhurst Park, 26 January 1993

Highest FA Cup final attendance (unofficial): about 200,000, Bolton vs West Ham, Wembley, 19 April 1923. An official figure of 126,000 is sometimes given.

Highest FA Cup game attendance outside the final: 84,569, Manchester City vs Stoke City, FA Cup 6th round, Maine Road, 3 March 1934

Highest Scottish Cup Final attendance, also a European clubs match attendance record: 146,433, Celtic vs Aberdeen, Hampden Park, 24 April 1937

Quiet crowd

The American football authorities once introduced a rule that required the home fans to keep the noise down to a particular level when the opposing team was preparing and calling their moves during a game. If the noise was too loud a penalty was inflicted on the home team!

Before the introduction of seating at stadiums, football matches attracted dangerously high numbers of standing spectators.

The aftermath of the Hillsborough disaster in 1989.

Spectator problems are not always due to bad behaviour. Sometimes the huge numbers arriving for a game can cause problems. There was an incident in one of the earliest Wembley football cup finals where so many supporters arrived to watch the match that they spilled over on to the pitch and had to be cleared before the game could start. This is why entry to the majority of large events is by ticket, and most are sold out in advance. There is careful monitoring of exactly how many supporters are allowed into games.

Several major disasters led to stricter safety measures at stadiums, including:

• Ibrox Park, Glasgow in 1971

• the Lenin Stadium, Moscow in 1982

• Bastia, France in 1992.

In the 1980s, two stadium tragedies occurred involving English fans that were to have a great effect on the way the game was organized in future:

• Heysel, Brussels, 1985 – a European football final between Liverpool and Juventus, was played at the neutral venue in Belgium. There were problems between the two sets of rival supporters and fighting broke out. Thirty-nine of the Italian fans were crushed to death when a damaged stand collapsed as they were trying to get away from the fighting. Following this incident English clubs were banned from taking part in European competitions for several years because this was only one of many incidents involving violent behaviour by English fans abroad.

• Hillsborough, 1989 – an FA Cup semi-final match between Liverpool and Nottingham Forest, at the neutral ground in Sheffield. There were problems caused by too many fans trying to get into one section of the ground. Fencing that had been put up to prevent pitch invasions meant that the fans at the front could not move away. As a result of this, many supporters were crushed and 96 were killed.

In 2006, England's Wayne Rooney was famously sent off during a World Cup quarter-final match against Portugal. Despite fans' disappointment at England's defeat, there was relatively little crowd trouble.

Football is not the only sport to have had problems with supporters. Riots have broken out during cricket matches and the crowd has invaded the pitch, causing the game to be abandoned. This happened in Pakistan when England wicketkeeper Alan Knott had scored 99. The crowd rioted and invaded the pitch, the game was abandoned as a draw, and he was denied the opportunity to score 100 runs!

There are even examples of damage being done to the playing surfaces. In one incident weed killer was put on a wicket to make it unusable. In another, the wicket was actually dug up.

Another notorious incident in football involved Manchester United player Eric Cantona. After being sent off during a match in 1995, he was taunted and abused by a section of the crowd, and by one supporter in particular. He retaliated by jumping into the crowd and attacking the man. Cantona was suspended for several months. The supporter was found guilty of threatening language and behaviour.

The problem of crowd behaviour led to strict measures being taken. Following the football disasters, the Government appointed Justice Taylor to head an enquiry into the safety of sports grounds and stadiums and compile a paper, known as the **Taylor Report**. As a direct result of this report, all-seater stadiums were gradually introduced.

There are also other measures in place to ensure safety and good behaviour at grounds:

- *Segregation of fans* the different sets of supporters are usually seated in separate parts of the ground and kept apart. This can also apply to fans as they are travelling to the game and leaving afterwards.

- *Banning of away fans* – some clubs ban rival fans from attending matches in some circumstances. The **governing bodies** have stopped sets of fans travelling to away matches if their behaviour is not acceptable.

- *Surveillance cameras* – most stadiums now have cameras placed around the ground to identify troublemakers. The system is usually linked to a police control room.

- *Increased police presence* – large numbers of police attend major sports matches to control and organize the fans

- *Increased numbers of stewards at grounds* – all clubs now employ and train their own stewards, whose job is to assist and control the crowds attending the matches. They not only watch the fans in their seats but also make sure that the pitch is not invaded and that players are not interfered with.

- *Seating of all fans* – this was considered to be one of the most important and successful measures in curing many of the problems that existed before. Clubs at the highest level must conform to this regulation in order to be granted a safety certificate that allows their stadium to be used. If a club cannot comply it is not allowed to play in certain leagues or competitions.

- *Better amenities and provision* – most of the amenities, such as toilets and refreshment areas, that existed at the grounds were very basic. These have all now been upgraded and many clubs provide entertainment before the games to keep the fans occupied. This is similar to the build-up before matches in many sports stadiums in the United States, where there is an extensive line-up of warm-up games and other attractions.

- *Specialized areas* – certain groups are identified by the clubs and given specific areas of the ground in which to sit. These can include children's enclosures or family enclosures where these groups can watch in safety.

Some of these measures were introduced to improve the image of sport and make it more appealing for spectators to attend.

The hooligan elements that had dominated in the 1970s and 1980s had led to falling attendances because people did not want to put up with the violence and obscene chanting that accompanied many games. The fact that football teams had been banned from taking part in European competition also reduced the appeal to fans.

Nowadays, football fans in the UK tend to be better behaved although incidents do still occur. The game is increasingly becoming an event families can attend. The changes brought in as a result of the Taylor Report seem to have made a difference.

Specialist stadiums are partly funded by the crowds who pay to attend them.

One-off games can raise large amounts of money but tournaments can raise even more. This is why there has been such an increase in different sports tournaments over recent years. All the different World Cups in the major sports usually run over a period of two to three weeks, often in just one country and sometimes in just one city, so there will be very large amounts of money paid by spectators to watch all the different games.

The Wimbledon tennis tournament is a good example. It is based at a single venue where there are 19 grass courts and 14 other courts. The site is only fully used during the Wimbledon tennis championship fortnight when spectators travel from all over the world to watch the top junior and professional players. Each year the All England Club (the organizing body) makes a profit of over £25 million from running the tournament! A large amount of this comes from the more than 450,000 spectators.

Finance

Spectators usually pay to watch a match and this can be a very large source of income for any club or organization. Several of the top football clubs have attendances of more than 40,000 for home games and there may be between 20 and 30 of these matches each season. With many of the supporters buying **season tickets** in advance this can bring in a very large amount of money. But many clubs are finding that fans cannot afford to attend all games.

Fans who attend major events don't just spend money on getting into the ground or stadium. They will probably buy programmes, scarves and replica shirts or hats in the club colours. They also buy refreshments. This all means extra money going to the clubs. This is true not only for the major football clubs and other outdoor stadiums but also for many major indoor sports such as basketball.

The indoor facilities in the UK are not on such a large scale as those for outdoor activities

Old Trafford

Manchester United completed improvements to its Old Trafford stadium and during the 2006–07 season increased the ground's capacity to in excess of 70,000. This meant that the club would average gate receipts of approximately £3 million for each home game staged!

(unlike the United States, where there are huge stadiums with artificial pitches) but some sports can still attract several thousand spectators. The clubs rely on these supporters to bring in enough money to finance them.

Outdoor fixtures such as horse-riding events, or even golf tournaments, do not have the problems of having to restrict their numbers so much – and they do not have to provide quite so much for the supporters. These events can attract very large numbers.

The money raised from spectators attending games and matches is not all profit. It can be quite an expensive business catering for supporters. The clubs have to meet many expenses to take care of them, including:

- *Facilities* – these may include toilets, food and drink, medical and other health and safety arrangements, separate family enclosures, lighting, heating, car parking areas, announcement systems and even large screens for action replays of some of the play.

This is in addition to the actual stadium or venue itself. Sport may be competing with other forms of entertainment. The supporters will want to watch in comfort and be entertained as fully as possible before, during and after the game.

- *Supervision and control* – with a large number of people attending, **organizers** have a great responsibility to make sure spectators are safe and well looked after. This means that the clubs must employ stewards and marshals (as well as meeting the cost of initially training them). They must also pay for the services of the police. The fans have to be escorted, or guided, to the ground, then supervised when they are there. They then have to be safely escorted out and sent on their way home.

The police have to be paid to do this as it is beyond the normal service they would be able to offer, and it is the home club's responsibility to pay for this. Often, the police fee is one of the largest bills that the club will have to pay – and the bigger the crowd the greater the fee!

Behind closed doors

One method of penalizing clubs with a bad record for spectator behaviour is to make their team play 'behind closed doors'. This means that the game has to be played in an empty stadium, so there are no receipts from any spectators and the home team players do not have the advantage of the atmosphere generated by their own supporters. This has proved to be very effective as it punishes the fans, the players and the club.

Many things can influence whether you have an interest in sport and whether you take part. Participation is generally encouraged because it is accepted that there are benefits to be gained from exercise. Taking part:

- can improve your body shape

- helps with the relief of stress and tension

- helps you to sleep better

- reduces the chances of getting illnesses and disease

- gives you a physical challenge to aim for

- tones up the body and the muscles, which improves **posture**

- increases your basic levels of strength, stamina and flexibility.

Exercise can be very social and sociable, since it can involve joining clubs and associations and starting up new friendships. There is no doubt that it can also improve your general health and well-being. This is one of the major reasons why participating in sport is so actively encouraged in so many areas.

School

An Act of Parliament in 1947 made it a legal requirement for physical education to be taught in schools. There were other things that schools could opt out of teaching but physical education was made a priority.

In 1988, the Education Reform Act again stated that physical education was to be taught in all schools in England and Wales. In March 1992 the details of what should be taught as physical education were made law in the **National Curriculum**.

The National Curriculum

All National Curriculum subjects taught in schools are governed by guidelines so that all pupils are taught a similar and balanced programme. Following the introduction of Curriculum 2000 in schools there was an aspiration set by the Government that pupils should receive two hours of physical activity a week in all schools. This is being constantly reviewed and there is even pressure to get this total increased in schools in the future. The Government has made a pledge that this will be four hours a week by 2010.

Attitudes to sport

Since taking part in P.E. is compulsory for all pupils, this is clearly one of the most important areas in influencing attitudes towards sport.

Because of this schools are bound to have great influence on young people's attitudes to sport and physical education. Being made to take part in sport may not always be considered a good thing. Many pupils resent being made to do something that they do not enjoy. On the other hand, if P.E. is taught well and made enjoyable and interesting it should promote a positive attitude in young people.

The attitude and approach of the P.E. teachers at school (and the other teachers who may be involved in some teaching of it or in team organization) can have a marked effect. A bad experience in P.E. can put somebody off it for life and this has been the case many times in the past. This is one of the reasons why in secondary schools the P.E. teachers are **subject specialists**, meaning that they are specifically trained to teach this particular subject. In junior and primary schools this is not always possible, because the groups tend to be taught as whole classes by one class teacher who must have teaching skills in many more areas.

Facilities

Another factor very closely linked with the school is what kind of facilities it has. A school with good facilities may be able to offer far more and enable certain activities to be played at a higher standard. If a school does not have a sports hall, for example, it is just about impossible to play volleyball properly. A school without a swimming pool will find it very difficult to make sure that its pupils can swim!

Some schools, including many of the fee-paying public schools, have very extensive facilities that can even include 18-hole golf courses and equestrian centres. Inevitably, they give sport a very high profile.

Schools of excellence

There are also various **schools of excellence** that are becoming more common and which have been set up by some sports **governing bodies** to promote high standards in their own sports. Some of these take full-time pupils, with tutors to provide the other subjects, but many are part-time, with pupils attending after they have completed their normal day's education.

Specializing in P.E.

Once a pupil passes the age of 16 and enters further education there are greater opportunities to specialize in sport and to follow sporting interests. The growth of P.E. as an examination subject (firstly at GCSE level and then at A level) means that the subject has been given even more importance at school. It is a relatively recent thing that it should be taught as an examination subject. It was in 1988 that it was first introduced as a GCSE subject that could be taken as a nationally recognized award.

The skills and expertise of the staff will also be important. Only qualified people are allowed to teach P.E. One of the reasons for this is the safety aspect, as some of the activities do have an element of danger or risk. Some P.E. teachers may have specialist interests and strengths on which they concentrate. Many professional sportspeople admit to having been very heavily influenced in their choice of sport by their P.E. teachers.

School is probably the first place where anyone plays properly organized team sport and where matches are played against other teams. The **extra curricular** activities, taken outside the normal school timetable, including practices and matches, are very important. Most schools have a great deal of this type of activity, and the pupils are encouraged to take part. However, since this is not compulsory, there is a large degree of personal choice involved.

Sport for everyone

The fact that sport is provided for everyone, mostly with free use of expert tuition, facilities and equipment, is one of the main benefits of school sport. All of these things have to be paid for when you leave school and have the choice of whether to opt in or out of sport.

There are other important influences, even while you are still at school. These also affect your level of participation.

A variety of sports are introduced to pupils at school.

Parents and guardians

The attitude of parents or guardians is very important. If parents are very much in favour of the benefits of sport, then they will almost certainly pass this attitude on to their children. There are many cases where children of quite famous sports performers have followed their parents' examples and played sport at a high level.

It is the attitude, as much as the ability, that can be important for parents to pass on. Parents can also help and encourage in other ways. These ways include:

• *Providing equipment* – many sports require specific equipment to enable you to play or

Footballing fathers

At one time Nottingham Forest football club had two fathers in management roles (Brian Clough and Archie Gemmill), with their two sons playing for their team (Nigel Clough and Scott Gemmill).

take part. It may be very expensive and demand quite a big financial commitment.

• *Paying for facilities* – using any sports facility is expensive and some may be more expensive than others. To be a member of a golf club, for instance, could cost several hundred pounds a year, plus extra payments for each round of golf played.

- *Transport* – one of the major problems for young people is that they are not able to transport themselves (certainly not over long distances), especially if they live in **rural areas**. This usually means that it is left to parents to find the time and the means to get their children to and from their chosen sports.

- *Positive encouragement* – this is crucial because without it young players are unlikely to carry on.

Not all parents take a positive attitude towards sports activities. Some can even actively discourage their children from taking part. This can range from writing notes to prevent them taking part in school P.E. lessons, through to stopping them from playing in after-school matches, or not providing them with the necessary basic kit and equipment needed to take part.

In some cases, even with a positive attitude, parents may not be able to afford the financial commitment involved. It can be very difficult for any young person to succeed in sport without parental support.

Many parents enjoy watching and supporting their children.

Peers

Your peers are the people who are the same age and status as you. To most young people this would be the group of friends with whom they most often mix. The influence that this group has upon them is often referred to as **peer pressure**. Your peers are considered to be one of the most powerful influences on you as a person, and peer pressure can be very powerful.

If a peer group likes to participate in sport and can see all the advantages and benefits that it has, it is likely that the whole group will join in and take part. However, it is very difficult for someone to go against the group if the general attitude is negative.

There will be other activities and pastimes that the group might like to take part in and there will also be the problem of forming relationships between the sexes, with girlfriends and boyfriends all making their demands upon your time.

Socio-economic status

Socio-economic status refers to your position in society in terms of the amount of wealth in your family, and your lifestyle. It is easier for someone who has no financial worries to participate fully in sport and they may have a wider choice of activities available.

Examples of this can be seen in the sports of horse riding and skiing. Without a horse to ride and the money to pay for stabling, grooming, training and transporting the horse to different events, it would be impossible to become a high-level showjumper. Similarly, without the money to pay for equipment and trips abroad to learn to ski, it would not be possible for a British person to become a high-standard skier. Even if they had access to a dry ski slope, they would still need to afford to pay for lessons, and would have to go abroad to practise the real thing.

In many other countries socio-economic status is even more crucial, as the financial gap between people may be even wider. In many developing countries there is great poverty, and the choice of sporting activities is very limited. This is one of the reasons why simple and inexpensive activities such as running and football are so popular in these countries and also why they are so successful.

In some countries different sports are popular in certain areas. In parts of the United States there is a very strong tradition of producing African-American boxers (such as Mike Tyson), and this is often in the very economically deprived **ghetto** areas. This is a relatively cheap sport to provide and to take up, but it does offer rich rewards if the boxer is successful.

Distance runners

Kenya has a very long sporting tradition in producing distance running athletes. This is due in part to the socio-economic situation that exists in the country. Many of their famous runners of the past first ran to get to school. There was no public transport and distances were great, so the only way to get there was on foot – several kilometres each way!

Availability and access

Not all activities may be either available or accessible to someone without transport links near by. Facilities such as ice rinks, or even swimming pools, may not exist within the immediate area so these may be activities that are simply not an option.

Living in a large city may give you an advantage in terms of what is provided. There may also be good public transport links, to enable you to get there to use them. If you live in a remote rural area these opportunities will not be so great and your choice may be severely limited.

The media

There is little doubt that the **media** is a very important factor in influencing your participation in sport. The media actually aim to have an influence and can be particularly powerful in shaping young people's thoughts and ideas. They achieve this in several ways:

- *Setting trends* – media coverage and exposure of an activity can raise its profile and then directly influence people to take part. Basketball is currently very appealing to young people and clothing fashions are even linked with it. Sports manufacturers will use the media to promote their products as fashion items rather than pure sportswear.

- *Creating role models* – the media often give a lot of coverage to certain sportspeople who are achieving success, or who may even be controversial. This coverage can encourage young people to want to be like their sporting heroes. Sports performers now achieve the type of media coverage and popularity that was only seen with pop stars in the past.

- *Promoting and covering sport* – all forms of the media cover sport, but television is probably the most influential. Television can lead to increased participation in sport if it covers events and activities that might not otherwise be seen. The increase in snooker as a participation sport came about as a direct result of a television programme called *Pot Black*, which started a huge growth of interest. Also American football grew as a worldwide activity as a result of increased television coverage in countries where the game was not previously played.

Sport and physical education is one of the fastest growing areas of activity in the UK today. Its many social and health-related benefits have contributed to this. Many people are discovering the positive benefits to be had from participating in sport. They are using their increased **leisure time** in ways that are both enjoyable and productive.

Gymnastics

Every four years there is an increase in memberships of gymnastics clubs throughout the world. This is directly linked to the extensive media coverage of the Olympic Games gymnastic events.

Glossary

agent person employed by sports performers to look after their interests in arranging sponsorship deals, transfers etc

amateur sports performer who does not make a living out of playing their sport but has a full-time job as well

apartheid system introduced in South Africa that separated all people in the country according to their skin colour

bid (National Lottery) formal proposal put together and sent to the organizers to get money from the National Lottery funds

boycott refusing to go, or take part in, a sporting event as a form of protest

break even when a business makes the same amount of money as it has spent (earnings = costs). This means it has made neither a profit nor a loss.

dividend money that shareholders receive if the plc they own shares in makes a profit

double hit shot played in a racket sport where the ball, or shuttlecock, is actually struck twice during the same shot

dual use where a sports facility is used by the public and a school and not exclusively by one or the other

elitism system of selection where opportunities are only offered to certain individuals, usually the best, or most promising ones

ethnic minority group of people within a country whose way of life is different from that of the majority of the population

extra curricular activities carried out after normal school time or in addition to timetabled lessons

gamesmanship very poor sporting attitude that is very close to actually cheating

ghetto area where people from the same sort of background or cultural group live, usually very close together in poor housing

goodwill where an action is taken as an act of generosity and not in return for a payment of money

governing body group of people who are appointed to manage how a sport (or other organization) is run

GP referrals system arrangement where patients are prescribed exercise as a form of treatment. This could involve making use of the local leisure centre.

grant sum of money given out by local authorities or sporting bodies

leisure time time that is left for a person to choose what they want to do, usually the time left after a day's work or school

media television, radio, magazines, books and the Internet

merchandizing goods clubs sell that are associated with the club, and which earn them money

minority group group of people in a culture who do not hold the same views, or possibly religious beliefs, as the main section of that culture

minority sports sports that are just emerging or that do not have a lot of coverage or participants

multinational companies large companies that trade in all parts of the world and which have a product that is internationally known and available

National Curriculum details of what should be taught in schools, at different stages, categorized by subject

national governing body organization that is in charge of a particular sport

organizers people in charge of an activity or an event

peer pressure pressure put upon you by friends or associates

posture position in which a person holds their body

private sector part of the economy that is not directly controlled by government. Sports facilities in the private sector usually require you to become a member.

professional foul deliberate foul made on another player to stop them from scoring

public limited company (plc) company that is owned by a variety of different people (shareholders) who can buy shares in it on the Stock Exchange

public sector part of the economy that is controlled by government. Sports facilities in the public sector are open to everyone to use.

recreation active and healthy use of leisure time

rural areas countryside areas or areas outside big towns or cities where there is not a lot of housing

school of excellence school that specializes in coaching particular subjects or areas, in this case sports, set up to encourage pupils to fully develop their potential

season tickets tickets bought in advance by supporters for all of a team's home matches

shareholder person who own shares in a plc

sledging (in cricket) fielders or bowlers making comments to the batters in an attempt to put them off or distract them

sling shot shot played in a racket sport where the ball, or shuttlecock, actually maintains contact with the racket and is not struck cleanly

Sports Council body that was set up and is funded by the government to oversee the many aspects of sport in the UK

subject specialist teacher who is specifically trained in teaching certain subjects

subscription (subs) amount of money that members of a club pay when they use a facility

subsidized receiving payment from central or local government to help with running costs

Taylor Report report, named after its compiler Justice Taylor, that was carried out after the Hillsborough and Heysel stadium disasters

terms details of an agreement or contract

urban areas large built-up areas – usually large cities or towns

walk (in cricket) when a batter knows they are out, they start to walk towards the pavilion, without waiting for the umpire to call 'out'

Find out more

Books

Making Healthy Food Choices: Food for Sports, Neil Morris (Heinemann Library, 2006)
Making of a Champion: A World-Class Sprinter, Clive Gifford (Heinemann Library, 2005)
Star Files: David Beckham, Paul Harrison (Raintree, 2005)

Websites

British Olympic Association: www.olympics.org.uk
FIFA: www.fifa.com
Football Association: www.thefa.com
National [American] Football League: www.nfl.com
Sport England: www.sportengland.org
Sports Coach: www.sportscoachuk.org
UK Sport: www.uksport.gov.uk

Index

accessories 15
access to facilities 6, 45
accommodation 15
advertising 12, 14, 16, 18
amateur clubs 20
amateur sport 14, 31
American football 18, 34, 45
apartheid 29
attitudes to sports and games 24–7

basketball 12, 18, 33, 38, 45
Beckham, David 21
boxing 27, 28, 33, 44
boycotts 29
bump balls 24–5

Cantona, Eric 36
charities 20
civil rights movement 28
clubs 8, 9, 13, 20, 21, 38, 39
communist countries 30
cricket 4, 15, 17, 18, 25, 26–7, 32, 36
crowd support 34

discrimination 28–33
distance running 44
double hits 24
dual use facilities 7

Eastern European countries 30
elitism 30
encouragement, positive 42, 43
equipment 14, 42
ethnic minorities 28, 29
event entry fees and expenses 16
events, sponsored 13–14, 18
executive boxes 21
extra curricular activities 41

facilities 4–11, 39, 41, 42–3
facility providers 8–10, 11
finance 6, 9, 10, 20–3, 38–9
football 6, 9, 12, 14, 18, 21, 23, 24, 26, 33, 34, 35–7, 38, 39, 42, 44
football pools 23
football stadiums 23, 35, 37, 39
Formula One 17
fund-raising 20

gambling 23
gamesmanship 24
golf 5, 18, 25, 30, 33, 39, 43
good sporting attitude 24–5
goodwill 17
governing bodies 13, 20, 22, 27, 37, 41
grants 20, 22
gymnastics 30, 45

healthy eating 11
Heysel Stadium, Brussels 35
Hillsborough disaster 35
hooliganism 35
horse racing 23
horse riding 39, 44

image 16, 17, 18, 19
indoor sports facilities 4, 6–7

Johnson, Jack 28

Kenya 44

leisure and recreation facilities 11
leisure time 11

media 11, 18, 23, 45
membership fees 20
merchandizing 21
minority groups 28
minority sports 13, 19

national and local government 22
National Curriculum 40
National Lottery 23

Olympic Games 14, 31, 45
outdoor sports facilities 4–5

parents and guardians, support from 42–3
participation 18, 40–5
peer pressure 44
physical education (P.E.) 40, 41, 45
'point scoring' 26–7
private sector facilities 8–9
prize money 32
professional clubs 20–1
professional fouls 26
promotion 45
'psyching out' opponents 27
public sector facilities 9–10

racial discrimination 28–9
racket games 24–5
recreation 10
religious descrimination 31
research and development 17
role models 45
rugby 13, 18, 22, 25, 27, 32
rural areas 11, 43, 45

Schevchenko, Andriy 21
schools 7, 40–1
schools of excellence 41
season tickets 21, 38
sexual discrimination 32–3

skiing 4, 44
sledging 27
sling shots 24
snooker 16, 45
social, economic and cultural factors 33, 44
socio-economic status 44
South Africa 29
spectator behaviour 35–7
spectator facilities 39
spectators 21, 34–9
sponsorship 12–19, 20, 22–3, 32
Sports Council 20
sportswear 14, 16, 19, 45
squash 24
subject specialists (P.E.) 40, 41
subsidized facilities 6, 11
Sunday sport 31
supervision and control of spectators 39
swimming pools 6, 10, 11, 45

Taylor Report 23, 37
television 15, 16, 17, 18, 19, 23, 26
tennis 14, 15, 22, 24–5, 27, 38
time-wasting and delaying tactics 26, 27
training 15
transport and travel 15, 43
trends 6–7, 45

UK Sport 22
United States 18, 19, 28, 30
unsporting behaviour 26–7

Wimbledon 22, 32, 38
women's participation 31, 32–3
World Cups 32, 38